# The Whole by Contemplation of a Single Bone

POETS OUT LOUD

Elisabeth Frost, *series editor*

# The Whole by Contemplation of a Single Bone

Poems

Nancy K. Pearson

Fordham University Press   New York   2016

Fordham University Press has no responsibility for the persistence
or accuracy of URLs for external or third-party Internet websites
referred to in this publication and does not guarantee that
any content on such websites is, or will remain, accurate or
appropriate.

Fordham University Press also publishes its books in a variety of
electronic formats. Some content that appears in print may not be
available in electronic books.

Visit us online at www.fordhampress.com.

Library of Congress Cataloging-in-Publication Data
Pearson, Nancy K., 1969– author.
  [Poems. Selections]
  The whole by contemplation of a single bone : poems / Nancy
K. Pearson. — First edition.
    pages cm. — (Poets out loud)
  Summary: "A collection of lyric and prose poetry about identity,
fragmentation, depression and addiction" — Provided by
publisher.
  ISBN 978-0-8232-7117-7 (paperback)
  I. Title.
  PS3616.E257A6 2016
  811'.6—dc23

                                          2015032624

Some names, characters, places, events, and incidents are either the
products of the author's imagination or used in a fictitious manner.

Printed in the United States of America

18 17 16   5 4 3 2 1

First edition

*for Elizabeth*

# Contents

ONE

selene's horse   3

molasses   5

*two stars keep not their motion in one sphere*   6

coming down   7

prairies   8

apology   9

sandy mush, nc   10

tibia   11

lullaby   12

there was no horse   14

erwin boyd   15

blackwater   16

the painter   17

early peas   18

hardwoods   19

poke sallet   20

maples   21

abrams creek   22

telemetry   24

not a drop   25

cast yourself unwanted   26

intransitive verb   27

earthworm   28

diagnosis   29

scenes 1 & 2: incidence code ix   30

starling   31

wasp   33

withdrawal   34

out & back   35

on behalf of a whole   36

TWO

provincelands   39

sand   40

bird in space   42

bonewax   44

*what's this blue called*   45

houston   46

opening day   47

the whole by contemplation of a single bone   48

the diagnosis   49

discourse   50

secretariat   51

mining   52

daylilies   53

sunflower, provincetown   54

houston   55

reader,   56

waiver   57

first you erased your facebook page   60

afterword   61

archive   62

## THREE

left for dead    65

documents    66

it was a swell fiesta    67

harris's color wheel    69

margalo    70

blackberries    72

aphasia    74

typeface elegy    77

disfluencies    79

eulogy    81

honey    82

hungers    83

mirrors    84

moons    85

lichen    86

brazos bend    87

generations    89

archive ii    90

and yet    91

north star    92


Acknowledgments    93

Notes    95

*How shall the question, "Where does the river stop and the sea begin?", be answered?*

—KANDINSKY, *POINT AND LINE TO PLANE*

# ONE

# selene's horse

I asked James,
càn you feel you're dying?

Can you feel the water pouring from the hose
turn to nothing in the grass?

James loved his big rigs.
I love the sweet metallic reek

filling my own gas tank.
All day the train

shuttles heaps of carpet scraps
through the wild blue phlox of Georgia

where James' oil truck exploded.
When Aristotle said there must be something

immovable in the animal
for the animal to move,

he must have meant James,
two years in a hospital bed.

Like the woman smoking on the new billboard—
for one whole week only half her mouth

opened in the rain.
The marble head of Selene's horse

hacked from the Parthenon
was shipped to England in "manageable pieces."

To see it is to see pain
bulging in a single vein.

James can't smile or blink.
Selene's horse—

exiled, perched on a plinth in the cold light of a museum.
That's one thing.

Then there's James, wide-eyed,
nostrils flaring.

# molasses

Home, I follow the roads passing the fruit orchards and the roaring white sheds of honey. The clouds—always inclined to thunder. The rain travels west from the mountains. I climb for hours never reaching the summit. Call it: across a distance of years, everything I long ago experienced but didn't. It startles me. The washboard ruts in the hillsides. The peach-flavored white lightning in a George Dickel bottle. For years I resisted. I didn't know how little I loved. The sour green sugar-juice trickling from the sorghum, the simplicity of folk implements. During the 100-year flood, the Sandy Mush lifted Smith Valley Baptist right off its stone foundation. The creek split east; the church stayed straight. Miss Jessie Ball stood on her tiptoes, holding a long hickory, and cuffed the blood out of her students, her desk floating downstream. Beavers survive the winter by eating the insides of their houses. I miss saying all those goodbyes, my cheeks pale from weeks inside a TV room. In the television version, someone digs up a suitcase. What they find inside the suitcase: a life stripping the fodder, cutting the heads off. The juice right on the edge of boiling.

*two stars keep not their motion in one sphere*

My hunger transposes everyday figures. The butterflies now diffuse and spiral. The proportional distances between stars. In the beginning the study of the heavens. In the beginning the greatest epic of all time. Dictated, they say, by a blind man to his daughters. My hunger is a tiny point on a photographic plate. It could be Vesta or the pupil of your eye. A scattered sheath of corn lights the Milky Way where Sagittarius aims his shaft at the heart of Scorpio. Midst golden stars we stand refulgent now, said Ovid. It's hard to move. Some hungers distort. Some rapidly move in parallel lines—

## coming down

Note the deeply incised, the extremely bristly, the long spikes, the
stalkless umbels in waste places, in cemeteries, in vacant lots. Coming
   down, I can't

tell if a speck is a raindrop or a vulture. Tracing the mirror,
I blink hard to make sure I'm real. Once, they knew

exactly how many elements existed. I've run out of gas or water or beef
   jerky.
My head is a canvas tent framed with a strong head wind. I disappear

every time I look for me. It's the same thing
with God. All those days walking alone,

I couldn't straighten you out, couldn't shape you into one thing.
In May, Element 117 was discovered—

the decay of evaporation, invisible deserts.
Everywhere a daisy, minus the soft white rays.

## prairies

To be continued,
two things happened.

The oldest daughter went blind.
The dog turned a circle and died.

There were other things too but by that time,
I had cried myself to sleep.

I knew a boy who would not turn his head to the left.
And a dog, who chased his tail like a fish in a bag,

day and night and day and night.
I worry

until you read to me out loud,
*the sun rolls over the edge of the world.*

This turns me inside out
like an orange slice. The meat of my heart fluffed up.

For want of light, the eye will shrivel.
If you tie up your arm too.

And so again, you read to me in bed:
*with hands clasped, they ran a little way—*

sisters on a prairie. In New York,
I followed a blind man, his hand

holding rope. For 26.2 miles, two men ran this way.
There are people like that and trees hacked to the heartwood

now growing leaves. It is quiet
when the book slides to the floor.

## apology

Expanses of silence could be evasion. Or my everyday chaos coursing you mute. I turn to the creek and the sky, virtual strangers. We all share the tight grid of myth. Twice I pray. Twice I beg. What's the difference? Six orange spots on a butterfly wing. 1,000 fingerprints on my cell phone. All this shorthand. I could be deadheading the ocean forever. If I could end a conversation without tearing up the future. In the morning I vacuum the commercial grade carpet, throw out the cheese, hard as a tooth. The rain hasn't stopped. It deletes the dust from the bean fields, the yellow flowers turning to gauze. The farmers tell me the hills around here are steep as a mule's face. At 4 AM, I get out of bed, wash my mouth with pure rubbing alcohol. It tastes like immolation. People who go to church around here are called "good livers." Tell me how. The rain is hard. I wish I had stuck to the old story: everything is beautiful now. The rain fills up yesterday's footfalls.

## sandy mush, nc

Everywhere is uphill.
I haven't followed a road that doesn't follow a creek

that doesn't turn into gravel.
The first emancipated slaves

to build a farmhouse and farm their fields
"freely" did it here in Sandy Mush.

Some are chased. Some are chased
from the inside out. Withdrawal is hell.

The backs of my legs creased with dirt.

# tibia

The fields calm me. Sometimes I think I'm over being sad.
I reach deep inside myself

turning over rocks—a crawdad in the gravel,
one claw up in the air.

We have to be nice to our deformations.
The largest stones in the field. A collection

is a cairn or a wall. A field is a space
in which every point has a neighborhood

of similar space. Sometimes I split
myself open and stretch myself

out. When I'm flat like this, you can see
where the glue would go to connect

the continents. Like a paper map
of the whole world. I walk out through the right edge

and come back through the left,
climbing over the same green cow fence.

On an honest map,
the extremes look larger. I want to show you

my shins, how the bones trace a path back.
The tibia absorbs the years of shock.

I've been running long distances
for 33 years. It's a difficult concept to grasp.

Language alienates the feeling, the intact moments.
The contact is always the same,

ball of the foot to heel of the foot.
Repeating itself is a pasture.

# lullaby

Sung drunk, lousy song
sung worn-out. Song

pitched from a pickup
behind the Public Works Building.

Sung drowsy. Swaying, sang
and spilled the song

broken by the dog I loved and could not keep.
Sung myself alone

walking home in my waitress apron.
Song snorted—stung. Bandage

from the wrist of my past like a fruit peel sticks,
sung scraping it off.

The wash and repeat cycle song
I spun. Bitter song buttered

on my stepmother's mouth.
Half-talked song,

my father to the screaming:
the shearer's hold-on to the kicking one's song.

Song: Enough.
Song song everybody knows one.

Song rewound like a butter's churn:
my teenage yearn. Returned. Song

like a star appears,
and like a star appears the same

for someone else from very far away,
song heard through the concrete walls.

Song I need. Song I need.
Song I need. Appears the song

like two yellow eyes in a drainage ditch
where someone lonely feeds an alligator.

## there was no horse

But we put him to pasture and I couldn't get my head around it.
There was the burden of spring—the bees, the ants, the
    bluebirds

lifting the earth high in the air, my mother suicidal.
The vet said, there will be no pain and the doctor said,

there will be pain forever. Days and nights I fed him sugar,
blew soft puffs in each black nostril. My father said, leave him

well enough alone. The rain washed him. The stream uncovered
Eugene King's ruby, largest in Franklin. I spread the sawdust,

the lime, slept in the fields where the purple asters
were parceled in pitch from the Union Carbide where our fathers
    worked.

## erwin boyd

Erwin Boyd bought 50 acres here in 1874 for $81.00. A freed slave, he worked this field the rest of his days, flue-curing his bright leaf, wet bulb or dry bulb, the leaves turning gold through the weeks. His children bound out to the county court. We're all watching re-runs. When the sun comes out, you can smell 140 years of hay; sometimes what's left decays forever. A lace of wind blows through the black and porous curtains. Don't we all like to believe in endurance? Down pasture, Boyd's home still stands, in the chimney—a little mountain of twisted limbs.

blackwater

When I broke through the woods I was clear

to the marsh. The frayed scrapes.
The lost tongues.

A foal folding on the water is how the light went.
"Necessary and momentary activations"

is what my cousin the ex-Guard says
about using a flashlight

after the Republican Palace became a U.S. Embassy
before we gave it back.

At dusk, there's the weft and the heap.
The birds trapped in a pant leg.

The reeds following the reeds, the wind-blown sheep.
Every idea we ever had

pushed out
on the bench press in his garage.

## the painter

They ripen at different times. The petals immersed in liquid. Collation is difficult. The elaborate array of medallions, the star-like cells, fibrous structures. The brush tip inside the foliated hearts. I search for traces of the lost, the contours of absence. My words cannot add to it. Explanation cannot alter it. Your hand strokes all the way across the plane of night. One is heartbreak. One an act of translating. I wake to find six new carpels, an evolution emailed in a Jpeg. Morning drips its yellow green down my neck. I walk to the field. What is it I dare? The cornflowers, the thistle, the unbearable largeness of color—only you, your torn pieces of silk water shivering over the white page.

## early peas

Butter yellow warblers in purple nettle, cows. There are times when I can see three layers of mountain ranges, all a study in perspective. The barns lean. Coming down the backside of Early's Mountain, I take the curves wide. By the end of the summer, I'll have something. Hands can make a summer something. I'll pick the lettuce and the peas twined on the stakes. Fireflies get stuck in the house. You should see how bright they make a room. Living hard is not enough.

# hardwoods

Every year I forget the hardwoods.

Which trees are which,
Which ones idle for awhile,
Which ones burn with fever by September.

Sweet tree, unpacking your blue red leaves.
Sweet tree, gathering ink.

*Why lifts she up her arms in sequence thus?*
Sweet tree, you heighten me

falling. Sweet tree, you cannot sustain me
fallen. Like the bee's plunge

into the hair
inside the ear
of the flower.

Oh honey bee,
I miss you, for one thing,

complaining all summer.
The trees get so quiet with their ruin.

## poke sallet

Aggregate pokeweed, a handful of gravel, a plate of deep-fried whitebait. Use only the young shoots. Change the boiling water three times. A dozen young waxwings drunk from the berries. Some died. Some dragged their wings in the dirt. This is what we enter when we are born. The mature roots, the purest poison. To keep working, I tell myself it's what we leave behind. As if the earth is desperate. Each leaf is entire.

## maples

begin or end with light or blight. Like a child or crop,

Virgil's Carthage, the fiery course of mange. Looking up through—
becomes a shirt entirely bled through. Falling to the ground

puts your whole soul into one thing found. I'm a child. They're stars
growing inward. That tight. The divided fattened by a homeless light

or hue. Shirt by shirt my father moves out. I'm through capturing
myself standing under them, opening my mouth

like I'm on a mountain road opening my ears. Sounds fold
underwater. Floating red leaf, are you the piece come off

or the piece left behind? Hold or yearn,
I possess an un-entire thing.

## abrams creek

My father spreads his seeds across the table—
*Start Indoors.    Plant April.*

Look at me with my pills. A handful of gravel. An hour mows
its shadow over the field

rippling near Abrams Creek. I've come home
to come down. The woman on the other side

of the Good Samaritan Hotline said
there's no shame in that.

Coming here is like walking through the corn
when the corn is high. Something departs

like hair in a sink. Still, I count my pills.
There's a system to coming off.

I keep crushing trying to cut in half.
The bathroom counter turns granular,

geographic like a tongue.
Near my childhood home is a place called Cades Cove.

There's Hannah Mountain, Abrams Falls, Gregory Bald,
white names for the Cherokees who first blazed the paths

for pioneers carting camphor and sugar. There's a meadow
and in the meadow a gravestone.

Nestled between bluets and stargrass,
the small headstone reads:

Alea & Alea
Feb 12, 1839

I trace the name that death had named again.
Who needs one name for suffering?

Here's the thing. I hid my hypodermic needles.
I let my best friend smuggle my meth in her vagina

while the airplane, that slow pinball flipper,
pushed us closer to the mushroom-shaped bell

dinging in Las Vegas. Who thinks
cocaine is something that lives

and stays someplace around midnight?
Whole nations expire like this.

Around dusk, Abrams Creek glints with bottle caps.
And all summer my sisters and I sang beside that creek

*One little, two little, three little Indians*
*Four little, five little, six little Indians*

How many dispersed like dust, here,
where the water leads to a corn crib

where the corn silk once wrestled
with the fire of Winfield Scott?

A highway cuts up through the Smokies.
Wheels slap through my childhood bedroom

like questions turned over and over
in the dozed and graded earth.

When Andrew Jackson said, build a fire under them—
When it gets hot enough—

The moon fries up the stars.
Traffic pours into Gatlinburg.

Then, I down my pills,
those drops of turbid water leaving cusps.

# telemetry

It doesn't come to me quickly. I have to run for hours, sometimes twice a day, to rest my mind about it. Running up a gravel road, the gnats thick in the sunlight, the shade uneven. The electric fence zips, the cow paths snake into the woods. A metronome, the way the electricity trips where a plant touches it. I grabbed the wire with my hand, screamed like I was possessed, a watery scream. A warbler. Small enough to get caught in a spider's web. When I finish, a single line of rain on the fence. To rest my mind on it, that faint imprint.

## not a drop

Inside it, the floodwaters sink. I'm stuck. Without you, I don't know how to get along in the woods. Petals so deeply cleft. Surface lines sucked out. Improvisation. Depressions. Years in them. My want is a culvert. How would I know how to channel it. There's loss at sudden flow. I'm better at separation, tearing loose the berm. On the grass, fledglings, their washed-out bodies. Everything torn clean. Not a drop of blood.

## cast yourself unwanted

To make a crumble. Blackberries oats butter honey lemon &.
Shave your legs on the back porch, dunk the razor in a warm
mop-tub of dishwater. Cast yourself unwanted. An electric fence
with roses, shin bones and arm bones white with salt. The calves
asleep in the grass. The milky creek where the drainage tunnels
converge, where the children swim, where the catfish feed. The
walk home from the blackberry bushes. Drooping jewelweed.
Doubt you'll ever find any as sweet again. And flour. There's flour
in the crumble.

intransitive verb

Abalones, the sweet red ones, swim from my hands.
Bright galvanic fish as small as an ion,

a star plucked from the belt of Orion,
knowing one doesn't need an otherness.

A star or a verb. That was my loneliness.
When I was a girl I thought God needed me

like Anne Murray needed me singing *You Needed Me.*
It was confusing.

Is it you or the back/slashing wind
tugging at my sentence's end?

Nights I feel a pull; a red bobber bobs in the deep.
Could some one stay after *sleep?*

# earthworm

The trees remember what grows back but I don't dream like that.
To know a distance I use my hands. I'm out of reach or touch. I
talk to myself. I say to the earthworm, Earthworm, I'm sorry for
all those years cutting you in half just to see if you would live.
The spade pitches four clear notes. You learn so much about the
lost when they are dead.

# diagnosis

Years after the hospital, I sketch it—my diagnosis. A tree diagram.
The most stable type: you begin with a root node. I connect the
nodes with branches. The "me" node connects two sub-nodes,
"child" and "The Mean One." I laugh when I write "The Mean
One." A joke, I tell myself. There are other nodes, but I'm tired of
making up their names.

## scenes 1 & 2: incidence code IX

In the first scene, she craves extreme violence. The oaks hurl iron marbles. I'm thinking slowly. I've forgotten why the police officer digs his boot inside my spine. The other handcuffs my wrists. All this blue nylon. All this complimentary concrete. When you lose your senses, you unlock something unused. The pavement blazes with oil; the clouds don't mature. I feel sorry for the therapist limping on red stilettos. The problem was time. My interior effaced. The police officers radio other police officers who race a third squad car to the parking deck. One says, "we got a IX." In the next scene, the woman is in one location instead of another. Nothing makes sense. The therapist bends down, her blouse opens or caves in. I can't feel my hands behind my back. A great actor begins her career.

starling

I dream I dream.
The way the un-medicated dream the way
they dream and wake
to tell and lose again their way:

the abandoned sequence, the lost margins,
the illogical piecing together:
the starling's song,
that little fool.

*


To hear myself as others hear me.
To hear the starling sing to me
in my speaking voice—
the dismantled shapes, the burning ghosts

it mimics:
Shut up.
You're a crazy bird.
Hello there?

*


I dream I dreamed
of flight
or dreamed of fire once wrung
with the hands

the hair turns to nothing
you can bury.
Three times I tried to rid my son of lice
with fire I dream.

\*

The little starling speaks
my foolish dreams,
the kiss I mimic the child I pretend I hush little bird
who devours

the intricate collision
of red ants I dream of swallowing of
the girl who swallowed a washcloth
just a small white hospital issue facecloth.

\*


The mangled tune, the mingled twist
of carelessness. I say and it says back,
I love you, little fool.
A hymn becomes you—

\*


I dream I dream the way
the starling dreams the way
the captive one recalls
the word's shadow haunting a wall, the key's rattle,

a stranger's voice—how it rips apart the empty cage
and joins together
inside my lonely throat
as notes—clumsy but a start.

## wasp

It's late I'm cutting I'm coming down kicking the oxy for good I slice the pink one in half with the Safeway pill cutter and drop it into Tuesday I slice another pink pill and then slice that half into another half hoping it won't crush under the built-in razor out here the fireflies blink in unison flying high in the mountain trees touching the stars I wet my index finger wipe up the pink dust on the razor's edge sucking the bitter dust like sugar pink pills and the halves of pink pills settle in with the five other kinds of pills I'll swallow tomorrow the pill vanishes beneath my tongue I'm trying to understand it such small poison a wasp back legs floating behind it knocks into the wood railing of the deck floats around doing figure eights it keeps coming back looking for the paper shell of its home the one I knocked down with a broom handle all evening I hear it a solitary wasp

## withdrawal

Like shingles on a roof. Falling is never planned.
Butterflies shiver on purple bushes. Monarchs migrate
in two directions; silk moths live only in captivity.
Butterflies siphon salt from the mud.

## out & back

The out & back is inborn.
The red leaf turns like a y,

gets a little wily near its end
repudiating winter

like a prop plane. St. Ex flies
over the cold tiles of the sea,

over the swollen grains of the desert.
I run the woods, the concrete scree,

the river with the ruin
of itself: how a stone sings

the windlass shanty,
the capstan slave's plea.

Oh, Southern town.
Past halfway, the signs un-rhyme—

    4-Closure,
    Prison Area

    Do not pick up hitchhikers

Hurt moves forward.
Atlanta to the sea. Winding back,

the smashed grass ticks
in my tread mark.

## on behalf of a whole

Mountains are collisions. Moving across the globe. A fingernail grows insidiously slow. Sunlight is composed of so many blinding frequencies. The air is restless, the wind moves counterclockwise, scattering. Something has to clothe the landscape. The trees tell us more about the rain than the sky. The saplings' emergence. That enigma. People say *one day at a time* means forever. I don't understand that kind of line. The story of life doesn't begin with tongues and claws. It starts with space, with water. Delicate skeletons, amorphous jellyfish. Reader, be soft with your judgments. The oldest of birds did not leave the trees, the trees left them. I'll admit I'm powerless.

TWO

## provincelands

A peninsula: light of three horizons. Sixty miles into the Atlantic, we return to the place where we lived years ago. The frayed blue carpet finally stripped, a curtain repaired, the old metal desk, two lobster pots, rust and salt. Salt and wood. Wood and paper. The Life of Someone on the shelf. If I could walk in a straight line but glacials deposit. Dynamic mosaic. Soft benthos. Ripple dunes and star dunes and parabolic dunes: our angles of repose. What yields and holds. Yield. You should have died, dear, they said, miles ago. Miles of de-saturated fields. Begin with the size of a crystal. Salt and sugar. Travel it. Taste it on your scars. Revealing age, solving crimes, soaking up the blood of combat. Liminal edge. Brief life. Milk and seawater. Every form reborn six times. What more is there to say. The ocean is deep. Some abandon their post and vanish before they ever enter.

sand

Sea plums rust sweeter
from wind and salt—the landscape's upper limit
winding up.     How far

from speech
the spiny shrimp

inside the reef's colon. The fish
you caught me

still carries one vein not yet opened.
Thank that, thank it.

\*


What would the earth
marginally capable
of moving its own plates
                    unlike the smaller static spheres

submerge from us? Grasses abundant?
Dynamic pigments, appendages in the kitchen light?

Your hand is a solvent I cannot touch. The window's basil—
soliloquies isolated to one familiar

fragrance. I miss bumping elbows by the sink. You and I
both swabbing cotton and alcohol
to remove the day.

\*


What white can texture my miswording?
Sand covers the hole. The tree cut
down by mistake. You thought the winter killed the tree

and killed what it wanted most
to lose a leaf or two
to take a break
from shading over all our mistakes.

*

A pinhole horse,
a matchstick halo—
how I remember you.
I was bothered, too bothered,
by three healthy siblings who walked into MD Anderson
to get their stomachs cut out,

a risk either way, but everyone had died of the same cancer
in their family. Or maybe it was the one girl

who drank a red cocktail swirling with liquid nitrogen,
"the dark side of a theatrical cocktail." Anyway all four of them
had their esophagus sewed to their intestines

and I wasn't aware you closed the door.
I think dry leaves form rocks in an animal's stomach

and the hartebeest tires easily in loose sand—the intermediate between
sea and forest, not a way out, not a way in.

# bird in space

*after Brancusi*

Child, what efficient breath
you imitate

drawing a bird
without feet or wings,

your chalk breaking
the sidewalk. All morning,

trees in the city open to speed.
Winter has come in the hurry

birds live in. Your mother
sits in a metal bathtub inside Walter Reed's

Warrior Transition Brigade.
Two blasts and just like that,

her legs burned off.
Child, you don't understand

what should be visible. What science
drawing a bird the artist knows. The field marks,

the essential red drops on the wing
flashing from the dead stubs,

the burned-over cattails.
Warriors sleep on the street,

on the blue kickers of garbage trucks—
crack whores, skanks, cum-dumpsters.

Ignore their scarred hands,
their spans of liver spots, child. Draw

with your chalk, carve the cold walk
into a highly tuned nervous system,

the stick-bird, the abstract fledgling
round with hunger.

The simple glyph speaks
by shifting half her head in the sand

where the bent grass blows down
a song. Child, see how

the face surrenders
to hollow resolve

in the white trunk
of rain. Child, hurry,

gently scrub behind the wet ears
of your bird

in her stone tub. The wounds soften,
the hands, the feet dissolve.

## bonewax

To stop my ribs from bleeding, doctors applied bonewax. Veins or a riverbed sunk beneath the surface of the sea—the invisible divined by crack or rift or wear. My wife organizes my vitamins on a plate. I exaggerate the contours of an apple, my stomach so full from gravity. It's like swallowing superlatives, the way self-pity renders the body. Heavy, the condensation when the night is cold, the way I muddy a friendship. The stream washes the road away once again. The divide between here and there, the long limb of isolation, what's promised when I swear myself to healing. It's a mess for everyone when the stream sinks back, reveals the wound it opened.

*what's this blue called*

*after Ian Hamilton Finlay*

The gannets
plunge

into the sea

*how blue?*        *how blue!*

what if

the heart's journey
were vertical

the horizon's promise—
fractured?

      *how sad?*        *how far!*

## houston

Crushed into two no more no three
circles venting into half circles bleeding over asphalt diameters
off-shooting wholeness

way past the lane, past the other trees, the brief intense ones
way past the avenue, past 610, past
the Joel Osteen Corporation

to the place where I recognize
I am not situated

inside the field where the catkins lift
like fault let go
and then, a little blame collapses

## opening day

My dog sees a bird,
barrels up through the trees from the truck.

On opening day my father's no longer a tourist
waiting underwater

for a parrotfish. I'm not a fan of fish, my father knows.
My first love was a turtle named Martha

named after the very last passenger pigeon
now stuffed with sawdust. My father is a lime green leaf that gets up

and walks away when you touch it
because he's really a katydid. I can't remember the name for this kind

of camouflage. When I think of Martha in Ohio,
perched in her wire cage at the zoo

I think of a ghost with a song
about a great slurry pressed into a single McNugget

like a spirit hardened into an urge
that disappears. Like dandelions

or egg teeth. Like the idea that goodness is beyond us,
not in us. The trees break

with our searching.
She'd sing a song about sewing our eyes shut.

## the whole by contemplation of a single bone

With a whip graft, one stroke of a sharp knife will do it. My
     father wraps
the scion to the paired branch of the plum tree.
I'm unsure we'll see fruit.

I don't trust construction made from rupture,
the way the break at the end of a line
is not yet shaped by gravity, the way the surgeon said

rib "resection"
though he cut my ribs off the spine.
Without the smallest bone in the body, we can't speak.

The velvet violet skins of sand dollars, Aristotle's lanterns,
five secret doves like three bones in the inner ear,
the hammer, the anvil, the stirrup—

we all need figures. Tide after tide,
I draw my name in the sand. I am haunted
by completion.

Ribs sing an uncinate song.
We all long, a crow remembers a face—
your jaw and the many hairs on your arm bone in the library

light. Some nights I read to myself:
*He was a Real Rabbit at last, at home with the other rabbits.*
Touch the uneven white

architecture of my chest.
There once was a velveteen rabbit.
*In the beginning he was really splendid.*

## the diagnosis

The stronger the barrier to enter a category, the more you value it. When I wake, all the colored birds wrestle in my ear. The first time I met you—it took years to make you—I feel I knew you before you were born. As if you were a lover. I hated myself for calling myself "we" though the diagnostic said MPD. *We*, a book about a nation constructed entirely of glass. We breaks apart. The geography of train tracks. Built like a skiff. A keel, a high flared hull, so many pieces. I'm shattering you. Names are just numbers. There is no hierarchy in We.

# discourse

The morning trees move without a sound
my blood flows.

Forgetfulness opens a space with each step
my mind goes

somewhere new. Out here, I grow
inside myself a discourse

dissipating, a sylph, a cipher, a shadow—
tulle, kimono, canopy.

secretariat

Go freely.
Parse the wind's wash.

Take a V-
cup drink inside

the mechanic's station,
the cherry-

scented urinals.
Then climb up to where the old horse sleeps spying

the yearling barn,
the foaling shed long gone.

At Belmont
there's no flag half-mast

when a horse dies racing.

## mining

I had four names and four voices infinitely different from my own. Doctors forgot their unifying motives. I burned mercury to separate the gold and inhaled it for years. Oh, I burned briefly. I carved my inner child with explosives. I trembled. The Chileans say: *the mine is weeping*—get out.

# daylilies

The plan is to run the hill from the barn six times as fast as I can. The rows of peach daylilies growing beside the old slave house have 24 hours in them is all. The Chinese call the dried daylilies "golden needles." My need to repeat. Tonight my wife says, You're poisoning your body. I count backwards trying to identify each poison, but it's dark. She opens the shutter of her camera. A cow moans. Her calf taken. The second hill—I'm dusk to myself. That fast. Love, love won't change me. The fourth hill, I'm feathers. In the moonlight, the strings hold the fruit steady. Three green tomatoes, one split, burst from the stem. I won't last at this rate. Point the camera.

# sunflower, provincetown

You've got your head down
like a horse
and when a horse lies down
the others stand
to keep a horse alone
she will not sleep
The moon
once gone
more go
October grows
Composite heart,
a lonely horse keeps turning
west, turning east I go
farther than I ever have or ever will
the horse teeth spill, un-tine
you stand alone oh,

floating spine

# houston

the hay-like grass,
the dog piss stays awhile

if the sky had a tongue
if the truncated bayous—

why, this little bird comes over
dislocated as heat lightning (not the real lightning)

not home, here,
not touching down anywhere

the bird, the grass-like hay, I said that,
but I don't know hay anymore

so far from it grass

reader,

Some guiding saint or ordinary insanity led me to you. All hearts are the same, save an ounce or two perishing. Synchronized clocks, white archipelagos. Pinker. Hume. Newton. The apples bred red, bred tart, super cluster bred. Though the planets remain intact. Every leaf is a whole childhood. Take my core. Or share my woe in winter.

# waiver

Of course, the tiny pastry chef,
held at the elbows as he broke through the ribbon,

was disqualified. Still, the Queen awarded the Italian runner,
Dorando Pietri, a small gold cup

for failing to win the marathon.

*

I dream less and less
about the snow-bent weed sprung forth,

my body lifted to its feet by an umpire.
I was fourteen when I watched women compete

for the first time in an Olympic marathon,
the year Scheiss, the Swiss hopeful,

hobbled through the stadium tunnel,
her torso twisted, one arm limp, one knee stiff

as a table leg, one lap to go as she counted
again and again her feet

rearranged like two notes
the tern rasps.

*

Miles—my one desire. I'm no Philippides,
no hoplite, no soldier. Not my brother

running toward fire. Starting, I look back.

*

Tell me what lights the planet between the feet
for all those miles? Some mornings I can only see

the sand inside my eyes, my own face blind to me.

*

Scheiss staggered, drooled, held the thick, white salt
of her cheeks in her hands, her blood—

an obsolete windmill
pumping the sea into drying tins.

*

The longest race I ever ran
was a dream I swam alone. I clung to a barrel. I cried,

Do I let go? How the star–red ants
dissect a catfish washed from water.

*

Benoit won the race Scheiss lost.

*

A runner approaches Mt. Whitney,
his last ten miles through Death Valley,

he yells out to a lone rock shaped like a pickle,
I want an elevator of corn, some ham.

*

In the back of the pack,
I walk, limp, lose my pace to blisters. Tell me how

a three-footed starfish
still turns a circle?

*

It's true—

I signed a waiver.
Go away now. Leave my body here.

# first you erased your facebook page

*for a.*

I'm not alert to silences like a child with no discourse
there is nothing left now that goes unsaid
you extracted your stump with your own branch filled the hole
with your root's dirt as if nothing and everything depends on
where they found you
how you died I try to understand
not recount
to mark the points of your arrival and departure
I select words to aim at
making the OED they had to get through four meters of cards
every three months about 9,000 cards per month their lives regulated
by the knowledge they had to go all the way from Abbott's booby to
bluestone by the end of March 1984 and from blue swimmer to Cape
Barren goose by June alone in the dark you climbed the stairs
to the brand new scoreboard the million dollar stadium where stars
    are born
what if there's no word
for goodnight in the jungle they say don't sleep there are snakes
there are snakes at twenty-three why I wish you were me
when I was you I was locked on the highest floor of a psych ward
I couldn't see anything inside
what did you see way up there before
you jumped
a swath cut for more power lines
the felled trees packing the holes with their own stumps?

# afterword

Thoreau counted nineteen
dead in the salt grass
necks broken
yellow breast fat still braided
in the cracked plate-glass
sweating above the ocean.
When the light goes out, the man goes out with it
The lighthouse keeper
runs down sixty-nine brick steps
in darkness
light turning
to smoke
steam turning
to frost
green moths quivering
on the cold plate-glass

## archive

Chain the horse to the fields through the years of yellow litter. String the burley leaf, thread the tobacco in the spicy air, the curing barns fired. Cut the heavy sand lugs, top the stalks of the small pink flowers on the stem. Suffer the "Green Sickness," the nicotine seeping into the skin. Days under cheesecloth tents, spread the butter on coarse bread, stir white sugar into lemon water squeezed for the farmhands. In the kiln, a rafter's sparrow, a pistol releasing from your father's limp fingers. His RC bottle drips in your hands, mother.

# THREE

## left for dead

When Beck Weathers goes blind and the Eastern light
fails access to a dream. When, on an Everest ice fall,

a few hours rest is all you need. When a few hours.
When a man breaks ice from his eyelid. When he lowers himself

into the warm, primordial soup
of his death. When his rope uncoils from the spiny ridgetop

of reason. When he's left for dead. When then, he thinks,
I should get up and disco and does. I was reaching a place

where my eyes hissed with the pain in my ribs.
I was breathing hard, climbing

in a busted-up stairwell where a sixteen-year-old dropout,
in another documentary, mainlines.

Here, he pounds on his mother's door for help.
You're killing me, mother.

And so it goes, by the movie's end,
the young Jim Carroll dumps heroin for poetry.

I was tired, searched for an old favorite of my father's—Hee Haw.
Life in a plastic cornfield. Minnie Pearl hollering Howdee!

And there's Archie Campbell, his back to the cold and faraway
woman with an ice pack.

He's holding a scythe. He's singing,
Where, oh where, are you tonight? Why did you leave me here all
    alone?

Then, he turns and blows a raspberry.

## documents

Open a thirteen-pound box of bills. The smell of the ink and bond, the thermal paper, heat and impact. All the friction of the past producing marks. Bills, redeveloping colors, comparisons, charts. Signatures like lace. Corrugated signatures. A name is a coast or a cove. Linear or segmented. Inside the box could be citrus, a blossom of perfume, The Story of A Decade. So many numbers, the flaps of area codes, fading return calls. What sickness costs.

# it was a swell fiesta

wrote Hemingway of Pamplona.
The gored bull—blood from his chest

the inner fire, a swiveling red sea grass
flanking an ocean liner—

continues to run. The bones,
the sugary meat rolled

around the bones, the pink lungs
wagging their crystal fur in the air

carry the maimed animal through the crowded streets
of red neckerchiefs.

A boy, his chest racing
with the banana yellow stripes of a jersey

gives a two-finger whistle—
a fox is dead in the gorse.

A coyote bristles on the barbed wire.
The snake seeks higher ground.

The wheat, crushed in its milk.
After the hail storm,

under one buzzing streetlight
a cat suddenly appears

like a mole you can't ignore. The skull-size ice.
The corner drugstore's window busted-out

as if the old shopkeeper had up and killed the robber.
In the end, a woman stepped on the gas

instead of the brakes. My grandfather
alone in the new apartment strips

a dozen screws putting up blinds.
Do you understand the urgency?

## harris's color wheel

I burn the journals, the collages, the paintings and sketches, the pages of poems and letters to myself written in all the hospitals. I carry armfuls of black and white composition books to the yard where the grass is most threadbare. The flames rise to meet the stars. A star diagram. The central hubs connecting the parts. Like Harris's color wheel, three colored prisms bleed into eighteen colors. Black is formed by superimposition. Everything built on what came before it suddenly collapses. The backbones of the journals fold in, crippling the entire network. The diagrams of all my personalities no longer clarify the relationship between the parts. A flame zips open a drawing. Two black letters meet in the middle, becoming one bright edge—

## margalo

Still I ask myself,

Was Stuart a mouse or was he a boy
the size of a mouse,

their second son? Sleep opens
her shining arms for the weary Christian

climbing up from the muddy riverbank
but not for me. This is the love song,

I go crazy without you.
The indoor cat, her nose pressed

against the glass door.
Endymion, his face turned up.

Why was this your favorite? you asked
after a whole summer

of you reading to me in bed
and then it was winter.

Still I ask myself,

Was Stuart a mouse who felt with a boy's heart
or was he a boy who felt

like a two-inch sailor
steering into the enormous cave

of a paper bag? Night speaks
the high-pitched notes

that rest below the throat
of words. My eyes are wet

and you're asleep.
Please, read again the page

where Stuart parks his roadster in a ditch.
Here, he talks to a man

about meadowsweet and holy thistle.
And so I ask myself,

Was Stuart a mouse
with a heart as vast as a child's

or a man like a beast seeking,
a man searching

the flooded streets
of his heart

for a little brown bird
with a big song?

At the end of the day, you begin—
*he was headed in the right direction.*

# blackberries

It's tough getting them.
The chromatic scale of black drupelets—

each a half-step note from reach.
Have I ever said a prayer that isn't tied to strings?

I thrust my hands through the inter-dental width
of thorns, those skeleton keys

hanging on the wrist of God. God forgive me
the people I've wounded

storming in
for the sweetest lump meat. You know how biting down

on a single seed
is a way toward something apart from itself? What I mean is

my hands are covered in juice.
Like a swift freeing itself from the darkness, flying in circles,
   swirling upwards,

let me back-up. God forgive me
the evenings I've wounded

storming out,
dusk licking itself in a corner.

They say God's love is like a seed
lighting itself.

Lord, I love my country,
the blackberry thickets

sucking in, spitting out.
Sparrow or swift, don't we all

fall into aggregate darkness
for something?

## aphasia

Cradle my tongue
like you hold my head some nights, my neck heavy.

The feathers in my throat—
the words have flown.

My tongue's trouble:
articulating its two-ounce heart.

I talk to myself:
Christ, I'm freaking out.

My thoughts are bound
to solid bones. A cormorant sinks

from a surface
I am not breaking through

but tied to
like two notes braced by a slur

my words confuse
a ligature no longer used.

\* \* \*

Reeds brush the oily bird trying
for a distant blue

I cannot touch.
I can't explain a longing for being lost.

My tongue complains, such self-extension
tires me.

\* \* \*

Paddle me toward a tendon of night,
away from the morning beating secretions,

the creatures underneath, an itch
on the surface. They speak with fire,

deeply, a viperfish's fin
dangling. My modifiers abuse

one thing for another.
In that darkness, it doesn't matter.

\* \* \*

On the horizon I drill together
pipe-oil-mud-pump, the derrick

blowing fire through the weeds. The pamphlet reads:
ask yes and no questions,

use visual clues, a layered painting—
yellow rushes touch me first.

Sea-blue distances my awkward gazing,
pulls me from the TV re-runs, the episode

where Chrissy moves to Fresno
leaving Jack and Janet misunderstanding each other in Santa
    Monica.

\*\*\*

Til now, I never saw a cow by the sea
crushing acorns

where there are no trees.
Its mute shadow is a drug I can handle.

Some silences are ligaments
between land and sea.

There are no roots.
A morning glory clings.

# typeface elegy

I paused mid-stroke
when I noticed a moon jelly—

glassy, pulsating,
an open-leaf clover in the center of its invisible bell,

the reproductive organs forming
the round cups of an alphabet,

each U holding the delicate matrix
of guts. Like a typeface—

to understand what it means,
it becomes transparent.

My fingers thread the saltwater.
The moon jelly swallows

the contents of its heart—
fills itself with the inebriation of itself

blooming absence.
Like a letter's counterpunch,

the space, the handle
where the shovel unlocks an empty room

for the small yellow bulb
of my hand to unravel in

the earth where a lilac now roots
beside my best friend's headstone. God separated himself

from himself to let us speak. See how
the arms, the sweltering stems, the tentacled serifs

surrender their attention to an invisible meaning.
On your last day, you threw words to the floor.

There they gestured like fish
spit-out to sand. Oh moon jelly,

the soul inside the blue cenote
of my body—          an aperture,

the empty bowl I packed so carefully inside a shoebox
shoved under my bed.

It once held oatmeal on a bedside tray.
When words cease to matter,

there is all this white space.

# disfluencies

Rising or falling
the flocking starlings
magnetize together on the edge

of criticality,
like all crystals forming
repeat a gathering

like the stutter I never recovered.

One syllable listened to again and again,
one cold song or letter
warmed over and over turns

the heart in so many directions.

All weariness
all collisions
of loop and line,
the "d" that halts the "do,"

the breaking lips of words cut off from the numb tongue muscle.

So unwelcome, so noisy, so damaging
to progress. Murmurations dye the dusk
coming down. I can't fly

straight from "w" to "where I'm going tomorrow."

Or the next day. My words are not space
or time that moves.
They prolong

like a panoramic delay.

My father tells me
to pull a trowel
through the dirt in a straight line,

as if all our desires emanated from one source, point to line, a seed
to a flower the size of a small girl,
her tongue in search.

# eulogy

*for grandpa b.*

Having never known you, my voice sleeps in a copse
from which the birds have flown

leaving the quick and the dead
silence of an airplane cabin

just before it hits the black water of the Everglades.
The morning headlines said

an airline attendant led Christmas carols
and a man gigging frogs upstream

swore he heard the ghostly notes
hover like mosquitoes over the razor-sharp swamp

where the naked and maimed passengers
struggled in the thick saw grass. You hanged yourself

from a curing pole, the continuous smolder
of bright-leaf swallowing the distance

between our two barns. Standing on the dais,
I'm looking at a meadow

blurred with the dusk of blizzard.
The wheat has turned to dust, the sheep, buried.

I rake hay until my fingers bleed
for the cow, frozen stiff,

her tail stuck out like the tongue
my heart can't find

the stillness in the forest, the hush before
the sweet concert begins.

# honey

frantic one, humming with high-fructose worry,
driving & fixing your face to God's music station,
fingerspeller, airlifted soldier, iconic spinner,
bearded vagrant sipping the sidewalk's sugar,
waxy servant, slick queen blindly texting in the tunnel
of the gum tree's cavity, dumpster diver,
short-fused stunner, hitchhiker, drug runner
straddling the border, prison guard,
petty beadle, Mr. Bumble, bullied one,
honey bee, gay child,
sleep now.

# hungers

The tallest corn, miles of it, taller than the corn in our garden, taller than the trees. The leaves never end. No silks, no toppers, no threads of fruit. T. says the corn in The Mush is GMO. Grown for sugar to feed the cattle. Silage corn. All winter stalks decay under tarps, the silage dried to discs the size of potato chips, stacked in silos. Like a country you can eat. If we could live on stalks, charred sugar.

# mirrors

We eat slices of pig so thin I can see through it. Lardo. Butter.
We eat olives and asparagus with red sauce and shrimp in garlic
wine broth and bread in oil. Everything in oil, even the pig fat.
We drink wine and I feel sexy and you have a stomachache and
we love each other so much it hurts to disagree about something
as small as okra. You wear a new tank dress and I, soft light-
blue linen. The sky is blue and clear, honey and lemon, the corn
whistling on our way to town. The horses slick. We were married
yesterday or eight years ago. I could be high. Between the trees.
I feel like swimming. To spoon the stars, collapse the sheering
insects. We eat lemon cake with olive oil.

## moons

I have a blue glass of water, a blue blanket. I wait for something
in an email, as if it's only a matter of an email. I'm the only friend

in my world awake. I'm the only friend in my world
who gets that tonight I think about all the pills at once.

The creek scratches and the cows moan. The email would say,
I get you. Like nobody else. A moth beats its wings

against the lampshade. If I had—if I knew—things seem dire.
They aren't. I'm in a bed painted with bluebirds.

A yellow-cream headboard. The lamp is soft.
The darkness, quilted. I don't believe you when you say

you miss me. I don't believe in "unwavering,"
though the moon rises each night.

## lichen

Move a beehive slightly to the left.
        The whole universe changes.

Gravestones erect on the hillside. The eternal yellow lichen. I
    move my finger to find my name. Centuries ago the bishop
    abandoned

Upper Case. Skins were scarped from the work of writing.
Or a man raked oyster shells to sell to the button factory.

A grain of lemon in your eye. Any sadness fills us. Touch the
    fungi, the lacy immortality. Sing *Awake my soul just as I am.*

## brazos bend

Wintered lotus,
wrung of your one-watt heat,

your leaves float, seeds release. I limp
on two feet. I need a pill, an opiate to flower,

to fruit, to fold up
my pacing at night. Where your wintering stems break—

a lever, the midpoint of remaking
where I hesitate. I zoom out to find

what seeps through
the saturated presence of you.

One vantage point outside the history
of multiplicity—one seed pod, then,

an ugly thing I hold
trembling. I'm holed in.

Dear seedpod, I would name you pain but pain named me first.
Dear seedpod, mimetic alien,

will you not reciprocate
my bitter sentience?

My lens limits God's largeness, the water.
Floating lotus, a man tells me your seeds sow flowers for a
      thousand years,

your seeds we eat, unmake. I alter myself
by saying my hurt is a light. How a light hurts—

a firefly in a pickle jar
will shake to kill its brightness.

In your pod's eyes,
an animal slept, rain arrayed, a yearning stayed.

If a dying gives freedom to reshape,
what form should my return take?

## generations

Breaking the level of sea—the field. The rusted blood,
the seed's yellow angles, the rough stamina.

Aisles and aisles of illusion. Unmatched rupture.
Every intricacy I labor over. I could blame that on you—

the hopeless spreadsheets, the failed experiments.
That I'll give up again. Anyway. Several float up.

The mismatched, the minute. Every flower.
It took twenty years to finish. The fruit trees.

You climb a ladder, see four generations burned-over.
There are tears on your neck. It seems wrong

to react with excitement. That I'll give this up.
The field. The yielding fruit.

# archive ii

Assay the gold with a black quartz, touch my mind to it. Touch my face with your broad, bald muzzle, your cart of siphoned pebbles wet from the miner's river. Refute my story, my instability, the imagined diamonds, the golden hay, my ceaseless bundling of days. Did she hold your yearling mane, the untethered wind, the winged seeds before the stalks were burned? Touch my face to her, that stillborn foal, my mother's grief. Pity the poor carthorse mute in the curing barn.

## and yet

Stay. Black crumbs
stroked through yellow butter stay.

Humble green beans, jeans
peeled away

to the floor,
stand upright

for a minute more.
Stay. Field-pressed flowers stay.

Fox, eclipse, glass of tea
dying red

through the back door,
please, one more.

For the horse thrusting
her neck through

to the moving hand of you,
stay.

## north star

First and brightest,
one shines in a suppurating field

of snow. One only knows
if one dreams

of freedom. Not all prisoners do.
One over a stadium

of leaves big enough to hold a child
is how big really?

Some nights
I wish upon and wish I might

remember, not relive. One shines over one sea.
The fur traders safely

trim each other's beards on a rocky shore,
those naked fires of long ago, and now

I find it's right there where
I left it leaving

home. The leaves curing,
the ditches burning—

pole star.

# Acknowledgments

"Aphasia" and "Hardwoods." *Alaska Quarterly Review,* Summer 2014.

"Starling." *Provincetown Arts Magazine,* Summer 2014.

"Lullaby" and "Blackberries." *Crab Orchard Review,* Fall 2011.

"Bird in Space." *Spoon River Poetry Review,* Summer 2011.

"Margalo." *Mississippi Review,* Spring 2011.

"Selene's Horse." *Sycamore Review,* Winter 2011.

"Abrams Creek." *Spoon River Poetry Review,* Fall 2010.

"It Was a Swell Fiesta," "Left for Dead," "Waiver," "Eulogy," and "Typeface Elegy." *Tusculum Review,* Vol. 6, Spring 2010.

"Black Water" and "Opening Day." *Hunger Mountain,* Spring 2010.


Tremendous thanks to Inprint and the Fine Arts Work Center in Provincetown for their generous support and to the Creative Writing Program at the University of Houston for the opportunity to learn from and study with a talented and dedicated group of writers, scholars, and teachers, especially j. Kastely, Peter Turchi, and Martha Serpas. Thanks to my editors, Richard Morrison and Elisabeth Frost, and to the artist Diane Kornberg. To my family, to Mary Barnes Fibich, and to all my dear friends, thank you for your love and encouragement. Finally, all my love and gratitude to my partner, Elizabeth Winston. These poems would not have been written without her.

# Notes

Many poems inspired by *A Field Guide to Wild Flowers* by Roger Tory Peterson & Margaret McKenny (Houghton Mifflin, 1968).

selene's horse: The head of the horse of Selene is an Elgin marble in the British Museum.

prairies: Italics & references from *The Long Winter* by Laura Ingalls Wilder.

*two stars keep not their motion in one sphere*: quote from *Henry IV* 5.4.64.

sandy mush, nc: Sandy Mush, or The Mush, is a real community in the mountains of western Carolina. Names have been changed to protect identity. I'm thankful for research done at the University of North Carolina at Asheville D. Hiden Ramsey Library Special Collections/ University Archives. "The Sandy Mush Chronicles: An Oral History" by Stephen Cain inspired many of the poems here.

hardwoods: *Why lifts she up her arms in sequence thus?* Titus to Lavinia after her rape (act 1, scene 4), in Shakespeare's *The Lamentable Tragedy of Titus Andronicus.*

abrams creek: "When it gets hot enough" refers to Andrew Jackson's quote about the Cherokees, "John Marshall has made his decision; now let him enforce it! . . . Build a fire under them. When it gets hot enough, they'll go."

starling: Mozart addresses his pet starling as "little fool" in the bird's epitaph.

"A hymn becomes you" is from the Introit at a Requiem Mass: "A hymn becomes you, O God, in Zion, and to you shall a vow be repaid in Jerusalem."

out & back: Inspired by Antoine Saint-Exupéry, from *Wind Sand and Stars* (1939).

*what's this blue called*: Title from Wittgenstein ("What's this blue called . . . Indigo?") writing about minimalism in Ian Hamilton Finlay's poem "First Suprematist Standing Poem." Italics are from Finlay's poem.

the whole by contemplation of a single bone: Title inspired by the quote:

> As Cuvier could correctly describe a whole animal by the contemplation of a single bone, so the observer who has thoroughly understood one link in a series of incidents should be able to accurately state all the other ones, both before and after

in Arthur Conan Doyle's "Five Orange Pips" in *The Adventures of Sherlock Holmes*. Italics from *The Velveteen Rabbit* by Margery Williams.

first you erased your facebook page: The details about making the OED are from John Considine's fabulous book *Current Projects in Historical Lexicography* (Newcastle upon Tyne, UK: Cambridge Scholars, 2010), 148. The phrase "don't sleep there are snakes" is inspired by Daniel Leonard Everett's brilliant book, *Don't Sleep, There Are Snakes: Life and Language in the Amazonian Jungle* (New York: Pantheon, 2008).

margalo: Quotes from *Stuart Little* by E. B. White.

scenes 1 & 2: Incidence code 1X: 1X is a police code for suicide attempt.

Nicolas Hundley

*The Revolver in the Hive*

EDITOR'S PRIZE


Julie Choffel

*The Hello Delay*


Michelle Naka Pierce

*Continuous Frieze Bordering Red*

EDITOR'S PRIZE


Leslie C. Chang

*Things That No Longer Delight Me*


Amy Catanzano

*Multiversal*


Darcie Dennigan

*Corinna A-Maying the Apocalypse*


Karin Gottshall

*Crocus*


Jean Gallagher

*This Minute*

Lee Robinson
*Hearsay*

Janet Kaplan
*The Glazier's Country*

Robert Thomas
*Door to Door*

Julie Sheehan
*Thaw*

Jennifer Clarvoe
*Invisible Tender*